Excavating Light

poems by

Diana Ewell Engel

Finishing Line Press
Georgetown, Kentucky

Excavating Light

*For the Ewell, McMillan and Engel families, especially for
Nancy McMillan Ewell and Milton Watkins Ewell, Jr.,
and for Clint and Claire Engel.*

*These poems spoke from your light and shadow, our lives together.
Where would we be without each other?*

ACKNOWLEDGMENTS

The author gratefully acknowledges the editors and publishers of the
collections and journals in which the following poems appeared:

"Blueprint Revised," "Tabula Rasa," *Open to Interpretation: Fading Light*.
    Kolosov, Jacqueline and Slade, George, eds. St. Paul, MN: Taylor &
    O'Neill, 2013.
"Bonsho," *The Visual Poetry Walk 2016*. The Visual Poetry Walk Project Staff,
    eds.
"Daddy," *A Gathering of Poets 2016*. Krawiec, Richard, ed. Winston-Salem,
    NC: Jacar Press, 2016.
"Walnut Heart," *Flying South*, no. 5, 2018. Lindahl, Caudill, Vincent,
    Morrison and Shar, eds. Winston-Salem, NC: Winston-Salem
    Writers, 2018.

Publisher: Leah Maines
Editor: Christen Kincaid
Cover and Interior Photos: Diana Ewell Engel
Author Photo: Clint Engel
Cover Design: Leah Huete

Printed in the USA on acid-free paper.
Order online: www.finishinglinepress.com
        also available on amazon.com

Author inquiries and mail orders:
Finishing Line Press
P. O. Box 1626
Georgetown, Kentucky 40324
U. S. A.

Table of Contents

I. *Twilight*

Tide Table

I.

An alphabet of broken shells
punctuates the plain of sculpted sand,
spells some cryptic warning.

We are beachcombers
journeying to the end of the earth,
sky bleeding into ocean
on the blue horizon.

II.

Mom's aged legs
test the curve of the beach,
feet cherry-picking each step,
sand-wind whipping
her ankles.

She bends,
peers at a fractured sand dollar,
its tiny doves released.

O weathered heart,
Prepare.

III.

Pointing to the crucifix,
she tells of the laborer
who drowned in the undertow
last summer.

The dune-anchored cross glints
celestial semaphore.

I remember her words,
"Never fight it.
Swim with the current."
How at thirteen,
a seizure sent me hurtling
into thundering waves,

and ocean,
wild mother,
carried me to shore.

Tabula Rasa

A twilight-glazed table,
cleared after each flurry of meals,
scraped of wax from years of dripping candles,
stands in the still evening.

My growing-up years,
starless nights on this porch,
a distant street lamp
the only glow—
I would lay my head against the dark surface
to escape a gnawing loneliness.

As I closed my eyes,
chair slats became plucked strings of a violin,
its plea sweetening the air,
the table expanding into an open road.

I ran down its sanded surface
into emerald shadows
of sheltering trees,
the night, my cloak of invisibility.

I dreamed of living
in a lushly bowered tree house
where the only watchful eyes
were those of squirrels and birds.

On the floor beneath,
I walked into fairy tales
as my brothers and sisters
ran into woods, built tree forts,
swung on grapevines.

Now my autumn soul
yearns for the extinguished years.
My family has gone—
mom, fending on her own.
Our lives, like birds,
seek nests beyond this porch.

But this smooth, cleared table
beckons me.
In the failing light
another narrative begins.

Walnut Heart

My wide-grinning dad,
you held out midnight mica,
rocks gathered on beach walks,
confessing you couldn't spot sharks' teeth
or sunset-hued scallops in the sand.

Black like the heart of the green walnuts
that covered our West Tennessee front yard,
plummeting near the rope and board swing.
When you pushed me, I would fly up
and back down to earth—
my stomach bottoming out
as my legs pumped into tree-paned sky.

Beach vacations
you would sit in a lawn chair,
daddy feet in the surf,
read the paper as we rode waves into shore.
What did we know of death
until you died
and we became seagulls
winging through morning
searching for the bright to fill us,
believing you would appear at water's edge
if only we would wait.

Now older than you,
I walk my dog through the woods,
stepping over knuckled roots,
treading the worn path
that circles Oak Hollow Lake.

In the call of geese crossing water,
I hear an ache,
remember pungent walnut husk
as scent of last night's rain rises
from the earth.

Blueprint Revised

Only this wishbone
of a tree, veins extending
from the earth's heart,
seeks the phantom light.

Animals are gone:
birds migrated far
south, squirrels
seized tree lairs.

Nearby houses once open
with the clamor of children,
cacophony of kitchen,
recede into shuttered darkness.

Winter lays a landscape
of silence at my door.

Morning: I listen for the wail of wind
now gone, moaning in passages
where dull-eyed moles tunnel
only to hit rock,

far from the gray light
limning my window shade,

a faint vista hovering
after the dark hours,

on the edge of day.

Broken Cradle

Wind gallops the nightmare to my door.

I hear their voices
for the first time
calling me.

Breath catching
in my throat, I remember
blood streaming
from my body's cave,
how a week of rain
followed.

I wandered the house,
visitor
to an abandoned dream,
whispering
in the nursery
as I faded
into yellow wallpaper,
plush carpet,
sunlit dust,
particles of air.

Wind wrestles awake
the past once nesting in my womb.
Their whimpers race
up my back.
The brood bawls
at my window.

I strip blankets
from every bed
to embrace each beloved
in my arms,
cradle my own aching frame.

I will nurse us through
night's haunting wail,
sound the low register chord
of our severed lives.

Witness Trees

Behind the train station in Belgrade
a frozen tundra of warrior trees,
their branches unsheathed,
rip January sky.

Limbs dress
in drooping scarves, charcoal leggings,
denim shirt, wool toboggan.

Dimensioned by ice, slant of light, shadow,
disheveled ghosts.

Trees hang clothing of Afghan boys,
mimic their stick-thin bodies,
refugee children who abandoned
their garments
to shower in the icy air.

Ice Storm

The ice descent
spoke a sizzling whisper
as we fell asleep,
my hand below your heart.
I dreamed ice encased our home.
We froze into statues while sirens wailed.

Evening had ebbed slowly.
Huddling in our frigid house
lit with holiday candles,
we'd pretended to be pilgrims,
our daughter resigned to school-required reading.
You dissed discontent,
tossed jokes into shadows.

Winter drives us
to Chivas Regal and Netflix,
worn cardigans to cancel cold's misery.

Outside, trees had split,
power lines tumbled.
I walked our dog
into spitting snow wind
of the rearranged world.

Unaided, an elderly neighbor wandered,
appearing confused,
slipped on slick road,
searched for home.

II. *Backlight*

Nostalgia

Think back
to long days spent
diving into
surf, emerging
with mouthfuls of salt
water, riding
thundering foam
into shore. Then falling
asleep, brain emptying
into the dark
of your bedroom.

Breathe in night.
Listen, tide.

Making Marbles

for my mother, Nancy Jean McMillan Ewell

Cleared yards, cracked cornerstones announcing family histories:
the lots we walked with you on Saturday mornings
as we excavated dirt-caked orbs,
flame and ice globes.

Sand, soda ash and limestone
melted into rainbows of glass,
these marbles were pressure-formed
in kiln caves.

You, fire-pressed in the kiln of a divided world,
streaking cap-pistol red, tree-jumping emerald,
colors coalescing in the air
gingerly exhaled by your reticent mother,
devoured by war-fatigued Dad.

Outside breathed frog-croak and high pasture peaches.
At the river, your walking stick
unearthed arrowheads,
vortexed the jetty's current.
This pattern echoed in wooded trails
became our inherited binoculars.

We tumbled down mazes of your making,
paths slashed through sleepy town days
leading to tree house and grapevine forts,
a wished-for white horse for Mike,
cedars cut to wear Christmas lights.

The stories you read aloud, forested
by wandering creatures, children,
stirred wonder.
Rackham's pond fairies,
Picasso's geometry
rendered our ore.

Our symmetries reconfigured,
we emerged as jack-o-lanterns
lining the eaves,
lanced the marauding dark
to open our sky.

Bonsho

Outside the temple, three bells swing.
First cast in wax, covered with clay—
earthen foundry
molded.
From silt to song,
earth to air,
echoing the ages,
ringing the divine.

An elder at her kitchen sink,
cratered hands scrubbing a rice pot,
turns off the tap
to hear the water of bronze.
In her vision a peal of light.
In her ears the echo of ancestors
singing in the hills.

Faith
for my sister, Elizabeth

Trudging trails of cancer's forest,
perplexed by hidden tumors and snaking turns,
she stayed with Joe, carried his pain.
Mind—intersection of fact and prayer,
light rending echoing silence.
Her throbbing temple
letter of love
as trail of crumbs dissolved
in rain.

She witnessed the cardinal
that no one else noticed
buffeted by storm,
grasping feeder perch,
ruby blur in downpour.

Grief

Drips into mouth,
hot salt curling tongue.
I'll sluice it into a dish
to rise like steam from cocoa
she made for us, mornings,
radiators hissing, calling us to dress.

Above the basin of my grief
rises dark-mottled moon,
startling fingernail
of crescent light.

Finding You
in memory of my father, Milton Watkins Ewell, Jr.

Your eyes reflected
morning quiet,
the steady spread of sun
to each green blade.

In this gathering dusk,
I remember you framed
in the floor lamp's glow,
your eyes penetrating
Bonhoeffer, Weatherhead,
the Interpreter's Bible
as you turn the page.

These books rest
in the oak bookcase
once in your office,
now in my guest room,
ask me to be still, listen
to know you.

Shadows whisper.
The potted hydrangea
droops blue clusters.
Outside, a young sparrow
looks for its nest.

You stay in your study
as I turn out my lights.
Moon polishes the room,
starts our conversation.

Backlight

Five a.m. full moon drops,
backlighting clouds that wander bruised sky.

Five a.m. moon falls,
the tiny amniotic sacs unable to anchor within me.

Our stubborn bodies,
those fallow years

embrace now on the driveway,
under the five-a.m. moon.

Our Braille alphabet—my lips caress your face,
your fingers stroke the nape of my neck.

This is how we map our affection,
our passion's ambit as the sun rises.

Later you will tell me of the mother wren
swooping into her nest on the patio shelf.

Hatchlings in this predatory world.

III. *Daylight*

Changing Weather
for my brother, Mike

I.
Do you remember
summers at Reelfoot Lake?
Cloud-high cypress,
long days, and water,
a still mirror.

You taught me
to skip a flat stone
I must flick my wrist and thumb...
one, two, three circles
growing wider.

How easy it was,
once I learned the technique.

II.
Out in the world
the unexpected greeted us—
my nightmarish pregnancies
birthing the ghosts of four children,
your twin boys,
wisps too weak to remain.

In dreams, I lay trapped
under the jon boat,
gasping, lungs filling
with water.

III.
Prayers for us,
orbiting birds,
winged heavenward.
We slogged through years,
lake glimmering,
memory of light.

In time thousands of blessings
brightened our doorways,
bluebirds that soared
through wind and rain
to reach us.
New friends, new purpose
nourished tired longings.

IV.
Now above the lake
dark clouds overtake the heavens.
Soon rain
will pummel the surface
and lightning, like fear, electrify.
Today, this deluge is mine.
I will stand drenched in the downpour.

Meet me at the lake, Mike.
Bring your smooth stones.

After the Blood Moon

we follow the wrack line,
our feet scarping tide-hammered sand,
past salt-eaten porch steps ripped,
storm's exclamation points fronting
pounded dunes.

Grabbing your hand, I suck in my breath,
laugh at how this feels like childhood—
learning how to ride bikes, this time with blindfolds;
spume-clotted water confounds sight,
revises the path, like friends and family,
beloved birds from sand dollars, crushed.

Two sisters make the slow sea-trudge,
into convergence where inlet and Atlantic meet,
to the isle of DeBordieu.
Our feet jam into underwater hills,
collapse into valleys.

Last push against the current,
we climb onto DeBordieu;
our legs trembling and cool,
western horizon sewn with sea oats,
pelicans lifting in a skyward V.

Our eyes, blood moons, reflect the late day sun.

Longing
for Clint

Sheets of rain
drum on the roof,
rivering across the patio table.

Inside my hope ticks
like a kitchen clock,
dissipating as each room darkens.

A truck engine sputters.
He enters, his eyes
halos of hazel light,

his legs, branches
of the only tree
I wish to climb.

Forest Language

Could I run through these needle-strewn corridors
until I reach the end of the world,
scamper up the sycamore's artery
skyward into a hawk's life?

The trails I hiked as a girl
echo now in walks with my mother.
Her mind ranges back to tomboy days
jumping pear trees in high pasture orchard,
sifting river sand for arrowheads.

We spy a great horned owl in fir tower.
Each falling leaf
letter of resurrected joy
landing in our path.

Daddy

Into the silence
I am walking.

In the silence
he opens the door

in the snow bank
of the river.

In his mouth
wait rescued outcasts,

behind his eyes
live tender-eyed dogs.

He is collecting leaves
and feathers,

making a bed
where we will rest

inside the snow bank,
inside the silence.

He will hold me close
and kiss my forehead

like when I was little
and he smelled of starch and aftershave.

The dogs will lick our noses,
all the outcasts sing.

Stripping Season/Note to Bill

Yesterday, after a month's break,
you smiled to greet me,
blue eyes, a smoothly-made bed
hiding memory's crumble,
voice steady as your gaze.

Today, cloth brace cradling my swollen knee,
I walk the wooded trail.
Roots camouflaged by November leaves
shanghai my feet,
force an attentive march.
I navigate treacherous terrain,
forfeiting lake glimmer and hammering woodpecker
as my eyes study the ground before me.

These legs are learning
how you could loathe your life—
confined to a walker,
powerless to help manage the house,
lately to pay bills, as the feared pit bull, for months
barking in train-whistling distance,
has charged the door, jumped your brain,
torn neat paper accounts,
digesting arithmetic and reasoning.

"A gift, a gift" cries a mockingbird
skimming opalescent sky.

I crane my neck, spy
hickory branches leaf-stripped,
now object of the sun's direction,
full throttle warmth soaking the bark.

You rest in the quiet of your room.
Light streams through the corner windows,
brightens your furrowed forehead.

Transformation
for Claire

1.
Snow, each silent crystal
glints design and purpose.
My daughter watches, wonders
as friends spin words.

2.
No corner can escape
this streetlamp's glare.
Laboring to banish compulsion's menace,
she compresses her bedtime ritual,
calms her nights into moonglow.

3.
Birds scatter as squirrels pilfer seeds.
Backyard feeder sways empty and abandoned.
Friends listen when she speaks her mind,
a welcoming cedar home for wrens,
bark resistant to harm.

4.
Wisteria climbs a clandestine trellis,
once in full bloom, invites the eye to see.
I quiver as her sudden soprano voice,
sweet bird, rises angelic
to balcony pews.

5.
Holding a rock in the darkness of Cape Royal,
she dwarfed the moon.
Finding her trail in the Appalachian wilderness,
she forges herself.
Now a dragonfly, she skims Shiraito Falls.

New Year Forecast

Following fitful sleep,
I wake to see the lightning-split elm
kindled-wet with winter sun,
skeletal arms shouting-up the sky.

My dark injuries
suddenly luminous:
Every tenuous misstep, loss,
small strokes on a canvas,
this landscape of light.

Like the sparrow at my feeder,
I can sing,
knowing the siege dies here.

My dog watches,
waits for my voice,
the stroke of my hand,
this familiar,
her treasure.

Special Recognition

I wish to thank my generous mentors. Poets Janet Warman, Marilyn Kallet and Mark Smith-Soto offered crucial insights and suggestions regarding the manuscript. Poet Ross White helped me fine-tune to success several of my chapbook poems. My verse reached a higher level as the result of North Carolina Writing Network poet Kathy Goodkin's astute critique.

Many thanks to members of Writers' Group of the Triad and Winston-Salem Writers poetry critique groups who helped me strengthen many of the individual poems in this chapbook.

A bouquet of sun-bright gratitude to Mrs. Jeanette Dean, a true friend and life mentor. Jenny gave me the precious commodity of time to work on my writing.

Originally from Dyersburg, Tennessee, **Diana Ewell Engel** has written poetry since childhood. She credits her parents for sparking her imagination in their choice of an Austen/Bronte-worthy house with a walk-on roof and windowed attic, a side-yard hosting the blue spruce she climbed to write verse.

She worked as a librarian in North Carolina for eighteen years before becoming a freelance writer and caregiver. With her husband, Clint, she experienced the rosy light of contentment as a new parent of their daughter Claire, and the haunting shadows of repeated miscarriages.

Her poems have appeared in *Asheville Poetry Review, Flying South, snapdragon, Wild Goose Poetry Review, Open to Interpretation, Perspectives, The Gathering, Wordworks, fire & chocolate,* and *The Visual Poetry Walk.* She created and taught a twelve-week *Verve of Verse* workshop at Penn-Griffin Middle School as well as several writing workshops, notably *Ice Melting on a Hot Stove,* at the Greensboro Creative Center.

As a volunteer, she has led workshops for Poetry GSO and Writers' Group of the Triad. She has served in many WGOT positions, as a poetry critique group facilitator and head of the *fire & chocolate* anthology project. She now co-facilitates a Winston-Salem Writers critique group.

Diana holds a B.A. in Literature and a M.L.S. from the University of Tennessee, Knoxville. She resides in High Point, North Carolina.

www.ingramcontent.com/pod-product-compliance
Lightning Source LLC
LaVergne TN
LVHW051608080426
835510LV00020B/3194